My Port

By Angus Olsen

For Ava

@idrawchildhoodcancer

I have a port, it looks like a little bump. It is very special and very important.

My port is under my skin, it has a tube that goes to where my blood is.

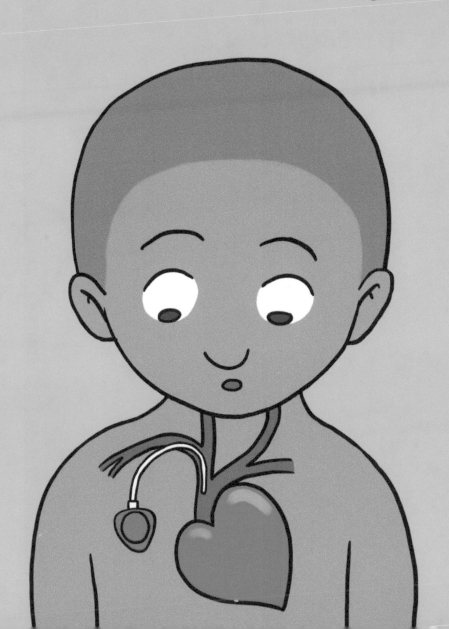

When it is time
to use my port.
A special cream
and sticky goes
on top.

I don't like it when the sticky has to come off to use my port.

The nurse says I am very brave.

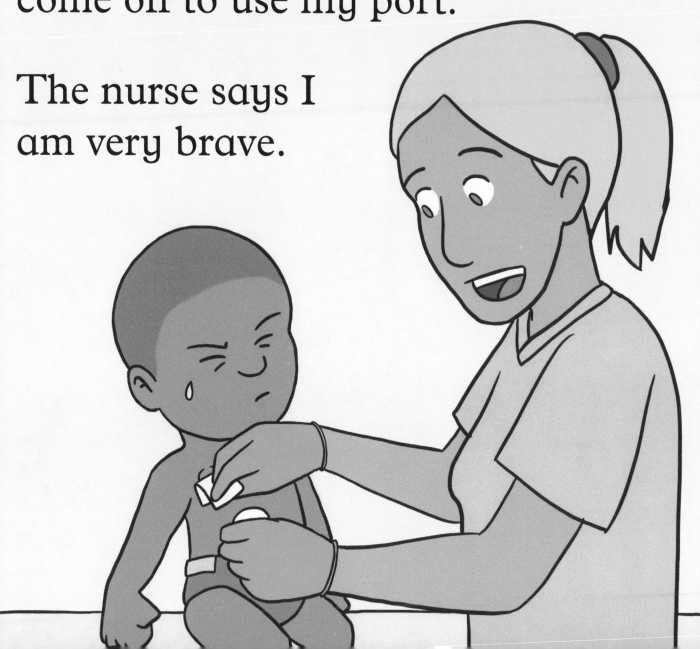

The needle looks like a butterfly.
My port can be used to
check my blood.

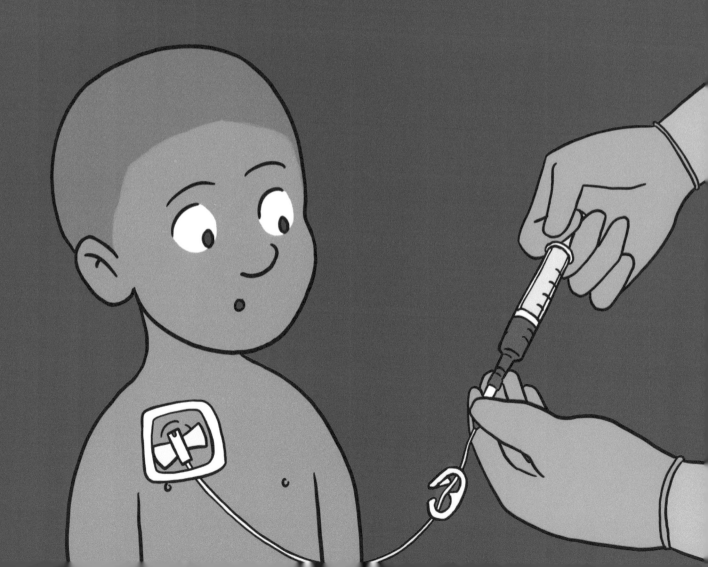

My port can be used to give
my body a drink.

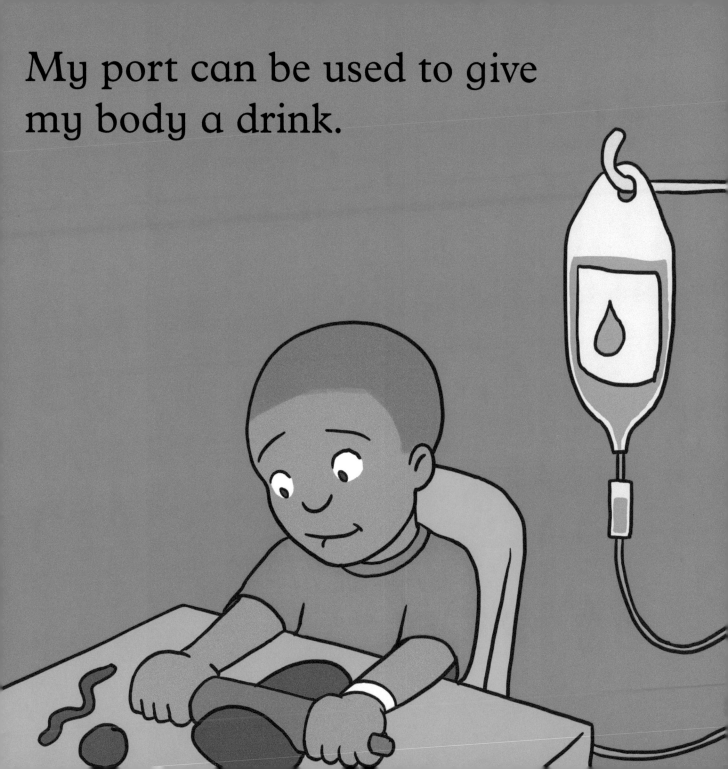

My port can be used to give
my body some medicine.

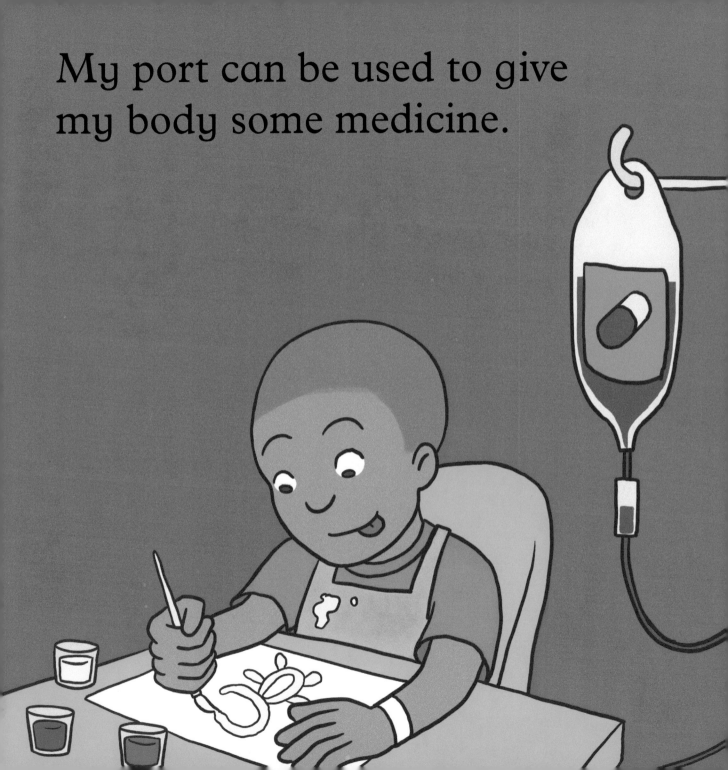

My port can be used to give
my body some blood.

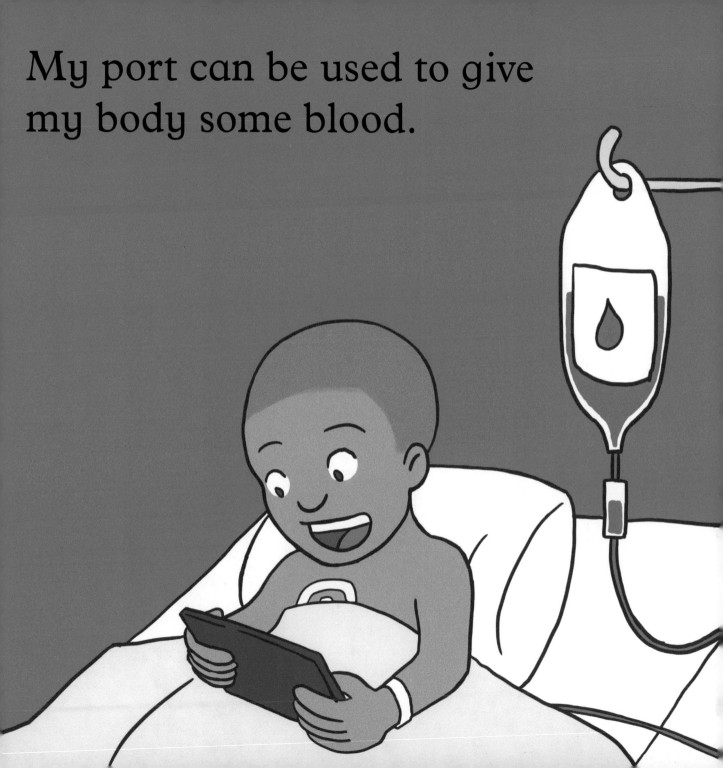

When my port is not being used
I can have a bath or go for a swim.

I have a port, it is very special and very important.

CPSIA information can be obtained
at www.ICGtesting.com
Printed in the USA
BVHW021155090322
631011BV00008B/22